NORT|

C000242502

10

circular walks
around the
Picos de Europa

Pete Ward & Trish Myers

black bee
walking guides

Acknowledgements

The authors would like to thank Suzanne Strevens
and Richard Beazley for all their help, encouragement
and hospitality at Olmares, Baseida-Lomeña.
For further information please visit
www.olmares.com

Maps reproduced under licence from the
Instituto Geográfica Nacional-Centro Nacional
Información Geográfica.

Whilst every care has been taken to ensure
accuracy, the publishers cannot accept
responsibility for errors or omissions or
any loss or injury sustained by any person
as a result of information or advice contained
in this guide. The terrain described is the
workplace for many, and routes may be
blocked or become impassable at particular
times of the year. The publishers would
be grateful to receive any comments and
can be contacted at the address given.

Written by Pete Ward and Trish Myers
Art Direction by Terence Keogh
Photographs ©Pete Ward
Printed in the UK by CPI Bath

Published by Black Bee Walking Guides
PO Box 197
Cirencester, Glos GL7 9AG
Email: info@blackbeewalking.co.uk
www.blackbeewalking.co.uk

10-digit ISBN: 0-9551286-0-9
13-digit ISBN: 978-0-9551286-0-8

NORTHERN SPAIN

10

circular walks
around the
Picos de Europa

black bee
walking guides

10 beautiful circular walks
Europa
in
Northern Spain

Contents

The Walks

black bee
walking guides

about th

The Picos de Europa National Park and the surrounding area is, in so many respects, a truly remarkable mountainous region of northern Spain. It is somewhat strange, therefore, that while it is well renowned it is, conversely, unheard of by so many.

The name alone – Picos de Europa – conjures up romantic historical images deriving, as it allegedly does, from the jubilant cries of the sailors in Columbus' fleet – as they returned from their expeditions in the Americas – on seeing the 'Peaks of Europe' and thus realising that they were almost home.

The region enjoys a supremely diverse and fascinating variety of geology, flora, fauna, climate, history and culture, about which many expert books have been written. This book does not set out to compete with these. It is, however, hopefully intended to complement them by providing opportunities to access and experience some of these features.

The authors are frequent visitors to the Picos having been completely smitten on the first trip some years ago and, like so many, we keep coming back to walk! There already exist a number of excellent walking guides to the region that we have used and enjoyed. A great many of

Tips and advice –
Landmarks and points
of reference – Code
of conduct

book

the walks described in these guides are, necessarily due to the restrictions of terrain and vehicular access, one-way routes – taking you from point A to point B. The authors recognise that these one-way walks are indeed the only way to access some of the most beautiful and remote places in the Picos but, by virtue of this feature, undertaking them means that some degree of extra preparation and planning is required to get you home. Broadly the options faced are: walk back the way you came, have access to two vehicles and drivers, organise a taxi or rely on public transport. The authors feel that for the typical visitor and walker some of these options are not always viable, especially 'out of season' when days are shorter and public transport is less frequent in the area or perhaps when language ability may be an issue. Equally, the prospect of walking back the way you came or scheduling your walk to a somewhat restrictive timetable will, to some extent, detract from a good day's walk – if that is all you want.

After long consideration of this we decided to research and produce our own guide to walking routes that have at least one feature in common – they are all 'circular'! Our walks may not take in the highest or remotest of places in the region, and, equally, if you are a

about this book

regular visitor you may have walked some of them, but the start and thus finishing point of each is easily accessible by car and all, we believe, are thoroughly enjoyable. Some walks are long, some short but on each we have attempted to include features of interest beyond just the fabulous landscape with opportunities to encounter the flora, fauna, history and local culture of the region. None of the walks are 'technical', difficult or precipitous – although most will require some degree of stamina and ability. The walks, although of varying distances, can all be completed in a day – some in an afternoon or evening, which is often a good thing at the height of summer or in winter.

The walking locations are all within an hour or so of driving from Potes, a pretty, historical town popular with visitors, from which all driving directions to the walks are described. While most walks are in the interior 'mountain' areas for a bit of variety we have included one coastal walk in the north of the region. Within the book we also include some basic, common sense advice and tips about visiting and walking in the region.

In essence the authors are two average walkers who hope you find this guide useful and that you enjoy the walks it describes as much as they did researching them!

TIPS AND ADVICE
Driving

The roads in the region are, in general, pretty good, many having undergone resurfacing and new Armco installation in the past few years. Some of the journeys to the walks are on occasionally steep and winding mountain roads so, while the views are splendid great driving care is needed. Even on the apparently main roads do not be complacent. Aside from the obvious safety considerations it is not uncommon for random speed traps to be placed in some of the villages and speeding fines can be high, often payable on the spot! Equally, be prepared to meet cattle droves – at any time of the year.

Summer Traffic: Los Llanos

When you arrive at any of the walks' start point park courteously, some have limited space. Ensure your vehicle does not cause an obstruction.

Climate

The region has a montane climate. As such it can, and often does, experience extremely variable weather conditions throughout the year. Generally the summers are hot and periodically wet; hence the reason northern Spain is known as 'Green Spain'. From mid-June to early September it can get incredibly hot – making midday ascents on any walk very demanding. After a prolonged period of hot weather expect thunderstorms – often of a spectacular nature and when it rains here in the summer, albeit briefly, it really rains! The winters at lower altitudes can be mild but extremes do occur. In early 2004 many villages in the Liebana valley, and elsewhere, had a metre of snow. Even in a mild winter, between October and April, there will be large areas of fallen snow at higher altitudes on many of the walks in this book.

After periods of frost this snow becomes extremely treacherous to traverse! If such conditions prevail the authors recommend you do not walk any of the routes described in this guidebook.

On any day throughout the year cloud and mist can descend in a matter of minutes placing possibly serious restrictions on visibility and thus navigation. Equally, daylight is an important consideration. In summer the days are long but in mid-winter there will be only about 8 hours of good light, even on a clear bright day.

The authors wish to make it clear that it is your imperative responsibility, at any time of the year, to take account of prevailing and forecast weather conditions before embarking on any of the walks contained in this book.

Equipment and clothing

While not definitive the authors would commend the following.

Comfortable, sturdy and, most essentially, waterproof walking boots are required on all the walks at all times of the year. You will encounter loose rock, marshy areas and streams. A spare pair of socks can be handy too.

Even on a hot summer's day carry an additional warm layer – jumper or fleece – and lightweight waterproof jacket and over-trousers, it can get quite cool at higher levels. This may seem unnecessary when the sun is blazing down on you in high summer but the authors have personal experience of being out on a hot June afternoon only to be caught in a sudden, freezing hailstorm! Not only painful and wet but also causing a sudden and astonishing drop in temperature of some 15 degrees Celsius – quite a shock to the system without some additional warm clothes. It is especially important to wear and carry sufficient warm and waterproof clothes in colder seasons and conditions. In hot weather take extra care protecting against sun and heatstroke. A wide-brimmed hat, high factor sun block and, highly recommended, a long sleeved top and lightweight walking trousers to protect the arms and legs.

Good quality walking sticks, while not essential and clearly a personal preference are, we think, a good idea. Not only will they help you traverse marshy areas and streams but also we find they do help significantly on some descents.

It goes without saying that, while also non-essential, you may miss much if you do not carry binoculars and a camera. We have included some blank pages after each walk for your notes and observations.

Maps

Spanish road maps are generally of the highest quality and accuracy, it is, however, a different matter when it comes to detailed topographical and footpath maps. Of the available detailed maps many are very out of date and, for some areas, seem to be non-existent or are very difficult to acquire at best.

By all means use a separate map in conjunction with this book but do take great care. Across the whole region lies a massive network of mapped and unmapped paths and tracks, some on common land some on private. On some of the walk routes described you will encounter a joining path or track that is not shown on your map. Equally, you may identify on your map a likely looking short cut or alternative route that may in fact no longer exist or be passable for a variety of reasons, most notably due to lack of use and subsequent overgrowth, floods, landslips, fallen trees, fallen river bridges and, occasionally, very intimidating barbed wire fences. Having encountered and checked some of these dead end routes the authors strongly recommend that you do not deviate from the routes described in this book.

The maps reproduced, with permission, in this guide are from the series Mapa Topográfico Nacional de España.

All of the routes described in this book were last researched and walked by the authors during December 2004 and January 2005. At these times all routes were found to be viable and passable – although with some snow at higher altitudes. The authors cannot and do not accept any responsibility for any subsequent natural events or human activity which may have permanently or temporarily closed the routes or made them impassable.

Sustenance

Here the usual rules apply. If you are a regular walker you will be aware of your metabolism and food and drink requirements.

Take food on all walks – sandwiches, fruit, chocolate, etc., perhaps a small flask of tea or coffee for cooler days, but, above all, carry plenty of water! Some of the ascents can be killers on a hot day!

Walk timings

We are not sure that we have ever followed any walking guide and achieved the precise timings it gives. No doubt this will also apply to this one. The walk timings we have given are guides and we feel include reasonable time for you to catch breath and take in refreshments en route as well as spending some time taking in the sights and sounds. Ultimately the time you take to complete each route will depend on personal ability, the weather and the time spent at any of the locations of interest we have identified.

LANDMARKS AND POINTS OF REFERENCE

The descriptions of the walk routes in this guide include a variety of generic types and kinds of man-made features as convenient reference points. What follows is a brief narrative description of some of these. If you are a regular visitor to the area you will no doubt be familiar with most.

Invernales These buildings are livestock shelters generally standalone but some beside enclosures. The older ones, seen in various states of repair, are constructed of stone with red tiled roofs whereas the more modern ones are often large breeze-block buildings with low flat metal roofs. They are to be found in all terrains from lowland meadows to mountaintops.

'Picos gate' The name ascribed affectionately by the authors for an old sprung bedstead very inventively used as a fence section or gate. Usually seen singly but occasionally a matching pair can be found – making an effective but quite surreal-looking double gate!

'Picos' Gate

about this book

Water trough (fuente) These are everywhere throughout the region and in all terrains, usually stream or spring-fed hence 'fuente'. They vary greatly in size and construction, from small utilitarian ones to massive commemorative affairs – the latter usually found in village centres; a fine example of which is to be seen on Walk 1. In spring and summer it is always worth having a close look into these, especially in wooded areas, for newts and salamanders.

Way marker The number of these basic but useful painted signs has increased a good deal in the last few years. There are two designations: white bar above red indicating a long distance route and white above yellow bar indicating a shorter route. The latter is the most commonly seen on the walks in this guide. They are to be found painted onto rocks, trees and purposely positioned wooden or concrete posts.

Way marker

Potro Originally a specific form of torture device, the name is now given to a simple, roofed structure for restraining livestock when being shod. Almost all are found in village centres, most made of wood but some modern ones are metal. A good example can be seen on walk 5 next to the forge.

Potro

Bolero These are outdoor skittle alleys on which is played the Asturian and Cantabrian form of ten-pin bowling. The surface of the marked out playing area is usually compacted sand. These alleys are found all over the region in towns, villages and even in remote locations usually next to the church or ermita. The best example we have found, constructed in 2004, is to be seen at Lomeña (Walk 6).

Bolero

CODE OF CONDUCT

As with any living and working environment, rural or urban, treat it with respect.

Mother and new born

Leave all gates and enclosures as you found them. You will encounter livestock on these walks – sheep, goats, horses but mostly cattle. All are passive but do not feed or disturb any and stay clear of a cow and her calf.

Dogs, in the villages especially, are endemic but after the barking has died down all will be well – 'bad' dogs are chained up!

And finally, as they say, leave only footprints and take only photographs!

the 'O

Walk summary:

Distance: Approximately 17.5 kilometres
Time: Allow 6½ hours

Description: This walk is titled the 'Old Lady' simply because that is precisely what the peaks of Peña Ciquera look like as you see them for the first time just after the 11-kilometre marker driving up the CA-184. Shortly before reaching Bar 'La Viñona' and the village of Pesaguero 'She' is seen, assuming clear weather conditions, on the skyline ahead of you lying on her back sleeping, or looking skyward, head left with the ridge to the right forming her body (see main picture above). Confusingly some locals also refer to her as the 'Old Man'. As you eventually climb up close to the peaks and under her 'chin', this image will have disappeared and she will become just another, but nonetheless impressive, group of limestone outcrops.

This walk initially ascends some 700 metres over approximately 6 kilometres from Cueva to the highest point of the route just below Peña Ciquera – the last part of which is a steady climb up a zigzag path to a quaint but utilitarian refuge. Then follows a fairly level walk through

Cueva – Peña Cíquera – Puerto de Piedrasluengas – Cueva

Lady'

meadows and beech woods to the mirador at Puerto de Piedrasluengas for some superb views. Finally there is a gradual woodland descent that follows a river back to Cueva.

Driving Directions

From Potes drive the short distance to Ojedo and turn right onto the CA-184. Just past the 16-kilometre marker take the right turn signed 'Cueva 3'.

On entering the village you will come to a plaza to the right of which is a rather grand commemorative water trough fed by 3 pipes. Ⓐ Behind this is the wooden potro. Here there is plenty of space to park.

the 'Old Lady'

The walk

The walk begins on the wide, upward track immediately to the right of the water trough that, after a short distance, follows a sequence of concrete electricity poles. After a few minutes and on the right of the track, you will encounter a fine example of a 'Picos gate'. Pass a water trough on the left and a large transmitter mast on the right ignore a path forking off right and follow the main track upward. You will come to a substantial gate across the path consisting of tree trunks slung between posts. Climb over or through these and enter a meadow. Immediately up to your left is an invernale and another directly ahead of you.

Head for the latter, aiming to pass to its right where you can just make out the path **B**. Pass through gaps in two fences, then, with the invernale close by on your left,

18

follow the path with a barbed wire fence and a meadow below this on your right, and woodland on your left. You will come to a small open area with a descending track joining from the left. Continue ahead through a wide gap into a meadow. Walking into the meadow turn half left and, follow the line of two large trees heading toward and passing close by an invernale, keeping this on your right. Over to the right you will also notice two other buildings in this meadow.

Continue on a narrow footpath as it drops down to join a wide track running left to right. Turn left and follow this track as it climbs and curves left. Down to the right may be heard the flow of a stream, Arroyo de Brez. The track descends and meets another track running left to right. Turn left and follow the track uphill. The track drops, fords Arroyo de Brez and then winds uphill through beech woods. Up left Peña Ciquera can be seen with a small group of trees growing incongruously in between the first two main peaks. ⓒ

the 'Old Lady'

The track, still climbing, veers right and somewhat disconcertingly heads west, away from Peña Ciquera. After a short distance the track climbs and curves round to the left once more, emerging from the woodland onto a large open area of grass  and rocks. The southwest peak of the massif is directly ahead and the start of the 6 or 7 zigzags that take the route to its summit at around 1500 metres. **D**

This is a good point for a quick break to recoup some energy before taking on the zigzags! Directly behind you in the near distance can be seen the parabolic peak of Peña Cigal, the home of a colony of Griffon vultures.

Continue ahead climbing up the well defined zigzag path as the views improve toward the north, behind you. Do not be tempted to shortcut the zigzags of the path, the terrain is very steep! Eventually, cresting the zigzags, you come to a large meadow sloping away. Ahead, in the far

distance, you will see the impressive tabletop mesa above Puerto de Piedrasluengas that looks as if it would be more at home in Arizona's Monument Valley. The path now continues down toward two small, grey buildings seen at the far left of the meadow ahead of you. ⒠

On your way down to these buildings you will pass a large water trough on your left, from which runs a black pipe alongside the path for some distance before disappearing underground. The first of the two buildings is a breeze-block refuge for livestock with a small wood and wire enclosure. The second is a refuge for stockmen. The legend above the door of this advises it was built in 1964. ⒡

the 'Old Lady'

Inside there is a very substantial fireplace, a table, stools and a large wooden bed. This is an excellent place for rest and refreshment, especially if it is cold or wet. When leaving please ensure the refuge door is bolted shut.

On leaving this point, and with your back to the refuge door, head directly across the meadow toward the peak facing you. Midway across the meadow, turn half left and head down toward the trees ahead. You will see a wide track heading into the woods. 50, or so, metres before entering this woodland track look ahead and slightly left above the trees to the near horizon. To the right of a small peak you will see a meadow with a track curving to the right. This is where you will emerge from the woods. While the track through the woods is very distinct it is not the easiest route. Numerous fallen trees requiring careful negotiation will confront you. At one point near a clearing on the left, with a large, concrete water trough, the track is particularly marshy. Emerging from the woodland, onto a rock-strewn meadow, the track forks – left and straight ahead, both of which peter out abruptly. Continue straight ahead across the meadow to meet a wide vehicle track. Follow this as it curves left round the hillside. There are views here to your right down into a valley that, during wet months and on sunny days, has myriad twinkling streams. As you come to a barbed wire fence and barbed wire 'gate' across the track look left into the

valley below. Down there, somewhere, is the final path that will return you to Cueva.

Pass through this 'gate' and continue along the track ahead. You will soon walk across a small grassy area passing two small concrete 'trig' points on the left. Keep straight ahead passing an electricity pylon on your right. The track shortly reaches an opening in another barbed wire fence bringing you out at the mirador at Puerto de Piedrasluengas beside the C-627. Turn left and head toward the wooden viewing platform. Ⓖ

The views from here, looking northwest down the Liebana valley with the vast backdrop of the eastern Picos massif, are stunning! You may not wish to dwell here too long though for during the summer months the place is understandably a mass of tourists and even in midwinter, providing the road is not blocked by snow, there may be a coach or two.

Continue your walk by following the wide vehicle track which drops down left of the viewing platform. Having followed this meandering track through woodland for 45 minutes, or so, another track joins at right angles rising steeply from the left. Turn and follow this track down immediately passing two white metal signs on the left; one nailed to a tree, declaring the land is both a national and regional hunting reserve. **H**

The track curves left and within a hundred metres or so a major landslip, which prohibits vehicles but is easily passable on foot, will confront you. Down on your right you will hear the rushing of the Rio Bullón. After crossing the landslip this distinct track now follows the river all the way back to Cueva. You may need to ford a couple of shallow streams running left to right across the track and negotiate a few stretches of mud, especially after periods of heavy rain.

Approaching the village the track drops down a short, steep slope passing a stone arch bridge, ford, small weir and 'homemade' wooden footbridge on your right.

As you come to the first houses of Cueva the path forks. Take either route – they will both lead you back through the village to the plaza, water trough and your car.

the 'Old Lady'

Notes and observations

a coast

Walk summary:

Distance: Approximately 14-16 kilometres (depending on your start point and whether or not you decide to visit the beach at Vega).

Time: Allow 4½ hours

Description: This walk offers a diversion from the others in this guide. It is lower level, the highest point being just 160 metres, in a generally milder year-round climate. The route intermittently follows part of the way-marked pilgrims' route to Santiago de Compostella. On this walk you can expect to see many wild, as well as garden, flowers and plants blooming or in fruit throughout the year. Although the walk begins and ends in a very urban environment it takes in some 'traditional' villages – which have both interesting small and large dwellings and many traditional farm buildings typical of the region. The walk passes through woodlands, mostly eucalyptus, and along cliff-top paths. While it is a great walk in all seasons it is perhaps best enjoyed out of season if possible, given that in high summer there may be many visitors in both Ribadesella and Vega.

Ribadesella is a medium size fishing port and resort town with a natural harbour offering good shelter against the worst of the Mar Cantábrico storms. It has a charming centre of criss-cross streets, a quay and a large central church and is well-worth exploring, should you have time.

Parking in Ribadesella may not be that easy, especially in summer and at weekends. There is a central car park with on-road parking beyond – beware of any restrictions – just past the turning onto the bridge. Alternatively, drive across the bridge and at the end turn immediately right and drop down onto the quay where there is also a car park.

a coastal walk

Driving Directions

From Potes then Ojedo drive north through the Hermida gorge on the N-621 to the town of Unquera. Join the N-634/E70 Autovia heading west toward Oviedo; eventually leaving at the exit signed Ribadesella onto the N-632. As you enter the town centre you will pass a large umber-coloured building, 'Mercado de Abastos', on the left and immediately after this is a left turn taking you onto the road bridge over the rio de Sella. The walk directions begin from this point.

Idolo de Peña Tu

The car journey also provides a convenient opportunity to stop off at Puertas de Vidiago to visit the ancient

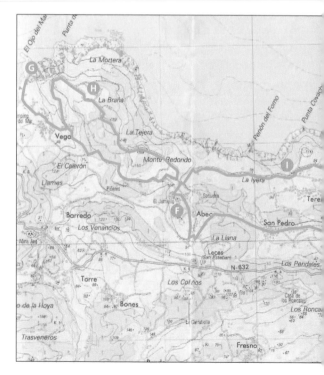

petroglyphs – the Idol – of Peña Tu. Directions for this are given after the main walk description.

The walk route

Please note: The map is somewhat out of date and, though the walk route indicated is accurate, much of the large residential area passed at the beginning is not shown on it.

The walk

From the Mercado de Abastos Ⓐ walk across the road bridge over the river following the footpath on the right side. Just as you leave the bridge look left across the road to see an 'hórreo', a variety of wooden grain storage

building traditional to this region, set up on tall stone stilts – 'pegollos' and 'muelas'; this is the first of many you will encounter on this walk.  **B** Continue along the main road and, just past a parade of shops and in front of the 'Hotel Derby', turn right and cross over the road.

After a few metres come to a stainless steel balustrade on the left and, as this turns left, follow it, joining a modern paved footpath that follows the Arroyo de San Pedro and soon passes a wooden footbridge with an elaborate tower near the opposite bank. **C**

You will now walk for approximately 1km along this path with the river and dense reed beds – a haven for wildfowl – on your left. On reaching a road, coming over a small stone bridge from your left, turn right and walk a  short distance to come to a roundabout. Take the left exit walking along the right side footpath noting, on the wall to your right, a marker for the pilgrims' route. **D**

You are now walking through a modern, neat but sterile, housing development and will, after approximately 1km, come to another unmistakable roundabout **E** having as it does an orange-hulled fishing boat at its centre! Take the roundabout exit straight ahead along a lane into more rural surroundings. After another 1km come into the pretty village of San Pedro. Late in the year there are a great many orange and lemon trees in fruit and, pleasingly, most of the modern houses here have been designed and built with a great deal of sympathy.

Continue along the lane out of the village heading up and passing a woodland glade where the stream runs down under the road from right to left. After another 1km reach the first few houses of the village of Abeo. You will come to a T-junction at which, on your left, there is a large wooden sign stating that this is a cyclists' route, turn up right.

Shortly, at a fork, follow the road as it turns up left. Follow this round to the right, noting the church over to your left and the mountains in the distance beyond.

Come to green painted metal railings on your right and, as these end, follow the right fork ahead, briefly down then up, with a road joining sharply from your right, toward a large, mainly white house dead ahead of you. Immediately opposite this house is a very 'sixties' style and rather uncomfortable-looking tiled seat. **F**

Just past this follow the road round to the left, indicated by a blue and white arrow sign on your right. Reaching a junction with another surfaced road turn down right passing a large umber-coloured house on the left and, after a metal-gated entrance to a field on the left, come to a white house on your right. Turn left here up a muddy track passing the first of a number of yellow gas pipeline marker posts on this next section of route. After a few metres, come to a fork. (You will return to this point later in the walk).

Take the left track following this up to some farm buildings. Pass with these on your right followed by a large clump of bamboo and continue along the track. At the next major fork keep left following the main track ahead and down.

As you emerge from the mature eucalyptus plantation you will come to a T-junction with a surfaced road running left to right. On your left at this point is an electricity pylon and down on your right a concrete 'trig' bearing another marker for the pilgrims' route. Most notably, however, you will see the sea and beach in the near distance over to your right. Turn right and follow this concrete road down into the village of Vega. Soon after entering the village you will reach a concrete track which forks up right past a house on your right, bearing the tiled number '11', opposite which is a stone wall bearing another marker for the pilgrims' route. Here you have a choice – detour down to the beach or continue the walk.

Vega is a small village but, because of its excellent, clean wide beach, becomes a popular destination in summer so at that time of year, especially at weekends, will probably be busy. If you wish to visit the beach stay on the main road heading down into the village until you meet a T-junction with a more 'major' road. Here turn right and walk the short distance to the beach. When you have had enough 'rest', or of other people depending on the time of year, retrace your steps back up to the fork beside house number '11' turning left up the track - from where the walk continues.

a coastal walk

Head up this concrete track, which is intermittently grassy, passing a blue-painted house on the right toward an isolated hórreo on the hillside. Over to your left, as you climb, there is an excellent view down to the beach at Vega G just before the track curves round right, high above the sea.

Soon you reach a fork in the track – down left and up right; follow the path up right. Shortly come to another fork, down left, up right; again follow the track up right. You will come to a stone invernale H set in a field on your left next to the track and, just beyond this, meet a muddy track running left to right. At this point you may encounter a frail 'barrier' to contain the cattle, possibly a white ribbon strung across wooden posts. Pass through this. Ignoring the wider left/right track, a narrow footpath is immediately ahead of you across a small, rough meadow toward a tall eucalyptus plantation.

Take this path and walk straight ahead passing through a gap in the brambles on the far side to meet another, wider, track running left to right. Turn left into the woodland. You may meet another ribbon barrier across the track. Pass through this and continue ahead. When you reach another fork, take the left and after 70 metres, or so, reach a wide, stony track running down from left to right. Turn left slightly uphill and continue. Another track joins at right angles from the right. Follow this right track, which can be very wet and muddy, through a young eucalyptus plantation although, on the

left, much of this has been recently felled giving views across to the sea. At the next T-junction take the track going left and slightly up. This winds for some distance with the sea on your left. Ignore all joining paths and continue ahead on the main track as it starts to descend, getting even muddier and steepish between banks on either side. Soon you will see a white house ahead of you as a track joins coming down from the right. Continue ahead toward the white house passing a yellow gas pipeline marker post on the right This is the point that you passed earlier on the walk. At the tarmac road in front of the house, turn left.

This road initially curves right then straightens out passing between open meadows for 1km or so until you reach the modern houses of Tereñes ahead. You will come to an urban road at its apex as it curves from your right and straight ahead. ① At this point follow a tarmac track immediately left past a brick-built rubbish bin compound

on your left. Follow this main track round right ignoring a track going off to your left. The track eventually passes between a high stone wall on the left and modern green wire fencing on the right and continues for some distance. As these end look up and slightly left to glimpse the top of the lighthouse, the cupola containing the light being atop a 'block' building. ⓙ Unlike most traditional lighthouses its effectiveness stems from the building's height above the sea rather than its structural height. Soon you will reach a T-junction with another tarmac road. Looking up left here provides a better view of the lighthouse. Turn right at this point. From here the road winds downhill for some 2.5 km, passing a large picnic area on the right, until it reaches the western end of the picturesque promenade above the beach. Follow the

seafront as it curves round, passing a number of impressive buildings on the right, the grandest and most decorated of which is the 'Hotel Cenador'. The balustrade along the sea front is decorated with crossed oars ⓚ and has a sequence of numbered entrances, or 'Rampa', onto the beach.

Dusk, Ribadesella

On reaching '3 Rampa' turn right, away from the sea, and shortly meet a road at its apex, curving from the right and ahead – follow it straight ahead. Just past an ornately glazed confectionery shop take a left turn, passing a supermarket on your right, at the end of this road you will emerge with the Rio Sella and the main town of Ribadesella ahead – the road bridge to your right. From here you can return to your car.

IDOLO DE PEÑA TU
Driving and walking directions

Driving toward Ribadesella along the N-634/E70 you will pass through the village of Puertas de Vidiago, approximately 15 kilometres west of Unquera. Off this busy road is the left turn for Peña Tu – the turning is small and not easy to spot. With the Santander-Oviedo railway running alongside the road on the right look out for a blue and white heritage sign indicating the turn to Idolo de Peña Tu. Take this and immediately meet a fork at which is another blue and white direction sign. Drive along the tarmac road between houses after which the surface becomes concrete. Continue as the road winds up coming, after 700 metres, or so, to an open area on the right that serves as the car park. From here, walk up the wide track for the remaining 300 metres indicated by a dressed stone marker.

Peña Tu is a large anvil-like limestone 'tor' on a hilltop above Puertas de Vidiago in an area where some 36 tumulii have been discovered. Unfortunately and in order to preserve the rock from desecration, a wide perimeter fence surrounds it, the gate of which is open year round during daylight hours. A smaller inner fence across the rock face gives added protection. There are no information boards but during summer months there is a guide and also the occasional costumed bagpiper – although neither can be guaranteed. Aside from the intrinsic interest of the rock itself there are great views out to sea.

Although a natural feature the rock bears distinct engraved images of human forms and more arcane images believed to date from the Bronze Age. Archaeological research indicates this rock was once an important place of worship that included ritual human sacrifice!

a coastal walk

Notes and observations

into the
Nation

Walk summary:

Distance: Approximately 17 kilometres
Time: Allow 6½ hours

Description: From Pembes the first section of this route will take you up into the Picos de Europa National Park, involving an ascent of some 620 metres to the highest point of the walk, in which area there may be an opportunity to spot the elusive chamois. From here the route picks up an undulating easterly and sign-posted track that descends into the pretty village of Mogrovejo. The route then heads through the smaller villages of Sebrango, beyond which there is a short but steepish zigzag ascent, Vallejo, which you pass below, and Llaves before gently descending back into Pembes. While some sections of this walk may be muddy and wet the last kilometre definitely will be – waterproof footwear is essential.

Driving directions

From Potes follow the CA-185 toward Fuente Dé eventually turning off right on the CA-888 signed to Pembes. Before this, just past the village of Los Llanos, notice the fields, trees and rocks to either side of the road

that are festooned with nationalist emblems. The man responsible, a self-styled 'Le Pen', frequents the markets in the area and is often to be seen with his decorated pick-up truck and goat at Potes market on Monday mornings.

As you enter Pembes the church and cemetery are by the road on the right. Parking is limited but there is some space by the church or close to the low wall opposite.

The walk

Begin by heading into the village passing a craftsman's house on the left, the front of which features many examples of his work; mostly agricultural implements. Ⓐ

You will shortly reach a house with a red brick balcony on the right where the road forks. Follow right and, as this road curves left and rises slightly, come to the village potro on your left. Turn right here heading up a short steep road coming to black railings ahead. Turn right and follow the road up as it leaves the village and soon becomes a rocky track. Walking up this track you will see ahead a small concrete water cistern with a masted solar panel; take the track to the left of this as it ascends.

After a stiff climb up this track, passing meadows mostly to the right that are abundant with flowers in May and June, you will come to a cattle grid and two

invernales; the legend on the furthest of which states it was built in 1965. **B** Continue ahead passing this latter building on your left. You will shortly see a much larger invernale ('Invernales de Vado las Aguas') in woodland beside the track on your right. Follow the track, with a valley on the left and woodland to the right. When you reach another invernale on your left, at the apex of a right hairpin, follow the track up right. After a short climb the land to the right opens up offering good views and, after a series of further hairpins, meets a fork. Take the left fork that rises and, on reaching another fork, continue up left – at about this point you have crossed into the Picos de Europa National Park.

You will shortly come to another fork, follow the track up left.

The path now rises steadily and straight for a while and up ahead you will soon see a modern, grey, flat-roofed invernale. Just below this the track curves first left, crossing the top of the valley, and then right. Ahead is a wire fence – pass through the wide gap in this and continue up.

Just after this point, and looking down left, can be seen the villages of Espinama and Pido far below. The track continues through a patch of broom and, emerging from this, meets a track descending sharply from the right. At this point is a walkers' signpost on your right bearing directions up right to Peña Oviedo and Mogrovejo and back to Pembes. **C**

The track ahead leads into higher national park wilderness and also to the upper cable car station of Fuente dé.

It is well worth spending a few minutes at this point – within a few metres of the highest level of the walk – not only for rest and refreshment but also to scan, with binoculars, the sheer rock faces ahead and left of you for a glimpse perhaps of the gravity-defying chamois that live in this terrain.

Continue the walk by following the easterly track up, signed to Mogrovejo, which soon passes through another gap in the wire fence previously encountered lower down. This track now winds and undulates ahead, passing the high cliffs of Pico del Buey above and a small wire enclosure on your left.

Passing a green gate and cattle grid the track heads down left and sweeps up right. After level walking the track descends toward woodland passing a wooden enclosure and water trough on the right. Shortly after this another track rises to join from the right, beside another signpost indicating that this right-heading route descends to Llaves. Continue ahead to Peña Oviedo. As this track descends it reaches a fork with more signposts, continue down right signed to Mogrovejo passing a stone water trough on the left – you are now leaving the National Park.

As the path veers down past rocky outcrops you will see the village ahead. At a signpost pointing back to Peña Oviedo take the right track eventually crossing a cattle grid and then a 'pink' coloured metal gate between posts bearing the white and yellow-barred way signs. Continue downhill into the village eventually passing by the impressive mediaeval Palacio de la Torre, **D** the ivy-clad sides of which you may have seen as you approached the village. Until recently all faces of the tower were covered but now two have been cleared to expose the masonry and decoration near the top.

Continue down the concrete road to the church. **E** This building has an external wooden staircase to the bell tower, below which is a covered cloister. There is also an information board with a map showing other important churches, monasteries and religious buildings in the surrounding area.

With your back to the church continue through the village, passing the 'Bar Mogrovejo', following the narrow path between farm buildings. Leaving the village and passing a back-pointing sign to Redo, you will meet the road CA-887. At the 1-kilometre marker take the concrete road that forks up right leading you the 500 metres, or so, to the small hamlet of Sebrango. Passing a modern, white bungalow on your left, an older building with 'car port' under it lies just ahead. Take the path that ascends to the right of this. Walk up this steepish zigzag track toward two transmitter masts. As you emerge from this onto a gravel area, these masts are immediately beside you and, with these on your right, follow the path as it curves round left down to Vallejo. Just below the village, in which many buildings appear to be ruined, the track swings left. Cross the stream running from right to left, continue along the concrete track until you come to a T-junction, at which turn left. After passing a church on the left the track descends into Llaves.

Shortly after entering the village there is a water trough beside a large stone barn on the left. At this point take the right turn and follow the track as it soon curves left, with a stone wall on the right and a series of concrete electricity/street lamp poles. It then ascends a short, steep gradient passing a white house on the left and water trough to right. Here the concrete expires and you are on a rocky track. After passing a fine example of a 'Picos gate' on the right the track forks steeply up right and less so up left. At this point the adjacent electricity pole bears two yellow painted arrows. Take the left fork and after a short distance come to the pebble-dashed building and aluminium mast of a television receiver station. Here, where a track drops away left; follow the main track as it curves round right below a rock face, from where you can see Pembes ahead. At the next fork take the track down left and descend gently through oak woods. Emerging from the woods the track curves left across a steep meadow, on either side of which you may have to pass through white ribbon livestock barriers. Follow this muddy track – often doubling as a stream in wet weather – as it descends, steeply on one short section between banks, soon turning sharply left and fording a stream. The track rises slightly after this but soon you will drop down to meet the road by the church at Pembes, at which point is a back-pointing sign to Llaves indicating a distance of 1 kilometre – it is actually 2 kilometres! **F**

Notes and observations

a Sho

Walk summary:

Distance: Approximately 6 kilometres
Time: Allow 1³/₄ hours

Description: Although a short and fairly simple circuit, both the walk itself and the drive (q.v.) to and from Cucayo have much to commend them. The walk, situated in a high and remote valley, is ideally suited to a summer evening or bright, clear day in autumn. Involving a gradual climb and zigzag descent, neither of which is too demanding and all on wide tracks, it is a good excursion for older, supervised children who will undoubtedly enjoy a picnic and the car journey. In summer the walk can provide a great opportunity to spot vultures wheeling around the crags above. The descent also offers something for those with a passing interest in geology.

Driving directions

From Potes take the N-621 toward Puerto de San Glorio. On reaching the major village of La Vega, after approximately 10km, turn left onto the CA-894, signed 'Dobres 11'. Passing the villages of Soberado and then Barago the road crosses a bridge and heads up through a

Walk

sequence of dramatic hairpins on one of the best mountain roads in the area. Just before the road enters the first of two short tunnels through the mountainside is the Mirador de Liebana on the left. This is well worth a stop, either on the way up or down, to take in the superb views of the road snaking down into the valley below and to the mountains beyond. After leaving the second tunnel the village of Dobres is on your right and shortly you come into Cucayo at the 'end of the road'. As you enter the village there is a bar, 'Peña la Prieta' (closed during winter months) on the left with some parking space beside it. As with many smaller and more remote villages parking here is limited.

The walk

With the bar on your left and the village ahead climb the wide track bearing up to your right from the road. Shortly you will pass a large, flat-roofed concrete building on the left (under construction at time of writing). At this point the track forks; down left toward a bridge, on which you will return, and up right. Take the right fork. 200 metres, or so, after passing a large outcrop of rock on the left and a cattle grid, you reach another fork in the path, take the

left fork. Following this you will pass a stone invernale on your right and then another group of buildings to both sides of the track. Beyond this you will hear the río Frío in the valley to your left. Shortly come to a larger group of buildings, Invernales de Ranes, where the river is more conspicuous. Ⓐ

Iberian green frog

Pass between these buildings following the track as it bears left crossing the bridge, Puente de Ranes. After passing the last building on the left the track ascends soon turning right, left and then right again at the apex of which a wide track leads off ahead through woodland. On the left a tree is painted with the white and yellow way mark sign. Follow this track. Pass a lone invernale on the left and then, as the track rises and curves right, a gate on the left with two more invernales beyond, the nearest having trees growing up where the roof once was. As you emerge from the woodland, a path joins

Homeward bound

coming down from your right. Continue ahead. After a short steady climb you will reach a point where the track forks, ahead up right and down left immediately to a stream, or streambed depending on the weather and season. Go down left across the stream and immediately bear left up beside a barbed wire fence to your left and an invernale close by and up to your right. Follow this path a short way until it reaches a T-junction. **B** At this point the high crags of Peña Ginesta lie ahead of you and, looking right up the track, you will see two more invernales. On a fence post immediately in front is another white and yellow painted way mark. Turn left and follow this track as it descends past an invernale on your left. At another fork in the track follow the path down left with a wire fence on the left. As you walk down this track Puente de Ranes, crossed earlier in the walk, and its surrounding buildings, can be seen down in the valley to your left.

The zigzag descent, viewed from the opposite hillside

This wide track now descends a series of zigzags ⓒ at the bottom of which it straightens to pass some impressive rock formations to both left and right. ⓓ

After crossing a cattle grid, then a river bridge, follow the track as it rises and rejoins the main track by the flat-roofed concrete building passed at the beginning of the walk, and drops back into Cucayo.

a Short Walk

Notes and observations

village traditions ar

meado

Walk summary:

Distance: Approximately 14 kilometres
Time: Allow 5 hours

Description: The overall ascent of approximately 750 metres, initially on tarmac and then on wide tracks, is mostly gradual but has a few short steep sections. On all the walks in this guide you are certain to see many flowers but this, perhaps, is one of the best when in May and early June the meadows below Obargo – before the first hay harvests – are awash. The village of Lerones has preserved many of its traditional rural and cultural features and has a most interesting church. This is an enjoyable walk for late afternoon/evening and benefits from a small but most welcoming year-round bar that offers a varied and traditional menu del día during spring and summer. All food is 'a la casera', literally 'of the landlady' – the fish soup, when available, is particularly good. Ⓐ

Be aware, should you disapprove of such activities, that in winter months Bar 'La Viñona' is the weekend meeting place for one of the biggest boar hunts in the area and where, when successful, the kill, often 8 or more, is laid out in the car park before the hunters disperse at dusk.

Bar 'La Viñona' – Lerones – Obargo – Barreda – Bar 'La Viñona

flowers

Driving directions

As with Walk 1 take the CA-184 from Ojedo coming soon after the 11-kilometre marker to the Bar 'La Viñona' on the right, beside which there is parking space.

From Bar 'La Viñona' cross the main road and head up the short, steep concrete track opposite, soon meeting a tarmac road at which turn left along the road, passing the right turn to Dosamantes. If you are walking this route in May or early June look out for tall lizard orchids growing on the bank by the roadside and in the meadows to both left and right. At a junction – to which you will return at the end of the walk – take the road left, signed to

Lerones, and follow this for approximately 1.5 kilometres. On entering the village a stone building ahead bears a hand-painted sign to 'la Iglesia' directing you right. Follow this sign and the concrete road up between buildings with the village centre to your left. At the first fork, by a water trough, drop down a few metres left to visit the preserved traditional village facilities. ⓑ First is the wooden framed 'potro', a device, seen on many of these walks, for restraining livestock when being shod, then the old council house, 'casa de concejo', the wall of which bears a modern but primitively executed blue-green plaque that identifies this and the other nearby structures. Next to this is a wooden door that opens into the fantastic 'fragua', blacksmith's forge, with its huge bellows. A little further on is the 'fuente', a spring-fed water trough beyond which, standing alone, is the roofed 'lavadero', the village laundry.

Walk up behind the lavadero and, with this to your left, turn half right and walk up the steep concrete road ahead, passing a walled and muddy livestock enclosure on your left, shortly reaching the church. Whilst this is usually locked the outside is well worth exploring having an interesting cemetery, gated entrance to the bell tower staircase and armorial engravings on the floor of the entrance vestibule. Looking up at the north-facing side of the church just below the eave you will see a somewhat macabre skull and crossbones set into the wall. These, reputedly, are the human remains of a former parish priest! ⓒ

Potro

Fragua

Plaque

Lavadero

With your back to the skull and crossbones the concrete road forks level straight ahead and steeply up right, follow the latter passing a 'farmyard' on your left containing some modern day agricultural implements. The ascending concrete road soon expires and the track follows a stone wall on the right. As this wall bears off right, you will come to an open area. Continue ahead reaching the wide track that soon forks, take the left track and continue up, quite steeply in places, passing a number of gates and pasture entrances to both left and right. In autumn the pastures to the right are often abundant with 'fairy rings' of field mushrooms. Looking down and right as you climb you will see the villages of Baseida and Lomeña across the valley and, immediately below, the red rooftops of Lerones. At a left curve meet another track heading down right, continue up left. **D**

You will reach a 'pinkish', metal gate that will be either open or closed across the track depending on the time of year. Pass through this and, although this is not private land and thus the gate ought not to be there, please leave it as you found it. As you reach a large, rough wooden post on the left, with barbed wire attached, the track forks down right and up left, follow up left. **E** At another intersection ahead of you is a reasonably modern-looking, breeze-block invernale beyond which across the meadow is another in ruins; follow the track going up left. On the hillside ahead can be seen the green roof of a long invernale, which you will shortly pass. Reaching another fork continue heading on the main track up left.

200 metres, or so, after entering sparse mature woodland the track, still climbing, curves right, at which point there is a wire fence with an opening into a meadow a few metres to your left. **F** From here are good views across to the Picos mountains. Rejoin the track and after a short distance meet a T-junction where the wire

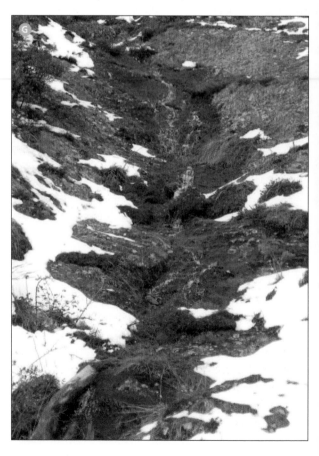

fence turns left. Follow the track right. Emerging from the woodland come to an open area with a small grey invernale over to the right and to the left the green-roofed invernale, mentioned earlier. Continue ahead, passing a long water trough to the left, as the track winds upwards along the hillside, intermittently bare and wooded with the jagged outcrops of Peña Porrera, at 1,265 metres, up to your left ahead. In woodland meet a fork, up left and down right, head down right.

Emerging briefly from the woods meet a ruined invernale to the right of the track and beyond this a small meadow. Continue straight ahead, and soon rejoin the track into more woodland.

Ignoring the track joining from your right continue ahead and downward, then level for a period, before descending more steeply and turning a sharp right hairpin bend. Continue down, ignoring a track forking up right, and come to a group of tall trees on the left where you will ford the shallow stream, Arroyo de la Rual del Valle, and follow the track as it curves left. Ⓖ

During periods of wet weather and melt water this point is the confluence of two or three streams that tumble randomly down the hillside.

With the large red and white-painted transmitter mast clearly visible ahead and below the path now descends into the village of Obargo. When you meet a distinct fork in the track head down right coming immediately to a recently built concrete water cistern, with solar panel, beside which the track surface becomes concrete once more. As this path drops into the village, past a large group of conifers, the first building on the right is the Ermita with two large tubular and one conventional bell hanging above its entrance. Ⓗ

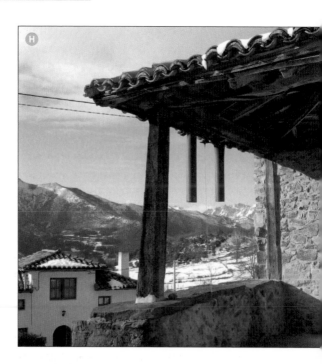

Turn right here and follow the lower road down, passing by a white house with green window frames, as it curves left to meet the 'main road' and, on joining this, turn right leaving the village behind. Soon pass green metal gates on the right, behind which, in spring and summer, is an immaculate vegetable plot. You are now heading

along a road, which passes meadows containing, during May and June, a vast array and variety of wild flowers including many types of orchid  and, standing above them all, large yellow, globular heads of lovage. Just past the first of two large, rustic wooden-posted and wire enclosures on the right is an indistinct track. As a brief optional detour follow this between the enclosures for a short distance into the meadows and to the banks beyond to encounter masses of wild lavender bushes.

Return to the road and pass a lone church on the left that, although built in the 19th century, has a rather incongruous breeze-block bell tower with non-matching bells.

The road now winds down, briefly up and then down again into the village of Barreda. Pass a water trough and lavadero on the right shortly followed by green gates into a farmyard. Follow the road right past a sign pointing back to Obargo. Barreda has a large dog population, none of whom are fearsome, so be prepared for a barking welcome committee as you reach this point! You are now walking on the main road and following this, as it curves left, shortly meet the right turn to Lerones taken at the beginning of the walk. Continue ahead passing the turn to Dosamantes and shortly after meet the steep concrete track that will drop you back down to the Bar 'La Viñona'.

Notes and observations

views fro
gree

Walk summary:

Distance: Approximately 11 kilometres
Time: Allow 4¹/₂ hours

Description: This walk is, above all, for a clear, cloudless day. While the small villages of Yebas and Los Cos are traditional they have no major aspects of interest – the key features of this walk, aside from flora and fauna, being the sensational views from the summit. The overall ascent from Yebas, approximately 550 metres, to the highest point of the walk is mostly gradual and initially follows a little-used track. While all tracks are wide and passable, some sections are a little overgrown with broom and one short section is quite steep. Walking sticks, camera and, especially, binoculars are desirable on this walk as is a wider area map and compass – neither of which is essential for navigation but will help to orient the views.

This walk has a second alternative start point before entering Yebas. This route climbs up beside a stream and then follows an indistinct and overgrown sheep track for 70 metres, or so, to join the walk route a few metres after point ❶ on the map and in the main directions. Instructions from this alternative start point are given at the end of the walk narrative.

Yebas – Monte Barcenilla – Corbera – Los Cos – Ermita de San Roque – Yebas ridge

Driving directions

From Potes head to Ojedo and take the CA-184 as far as Bar la Viñona, as per walk 5. Immediately after passing this turn right onto the CA-875, signed to Yebas. A good condition, winding road that passes the villages of Basieda and then Lomeña where the tarmac becomes concrete passing narrowly through the village but emerges the other side as a reasonable surface again. As you leave the village note the long wall to your left above which is a very grand 'floodlit' bolero constructed in 2004. You will have a better view of this on the drive back. A kilometre, or so, beyond Lomeña the road makes a sharp left, by a picnic bench and television receiver station on the right, and the village of Yebas lies ahead. The road then descends and turns sharp right to cross two small bridges each with pinkish orange railings. Just past the second of these, on the left is a small 'lay by' with one or more dustbins; park here – at this point also is the village name board and the road forks; the right fork taking the route through the 'lower' village.

The walk

Follow the upper road as it enters the village and passes 'underneath' a house ahead of you. Ⓐ After which it briefly descends then rises between a couple of houses, to leave the village and head toward a meadow. Follow this 'tractor' track as it takes a sharp left near some mature conifers, often used as shelter for the tractors, with a wire fence on the right, the surface becoming rocky, and enter more conifers. Emerging from these cross a small meadow heading first into a eucalyptus plantation, then

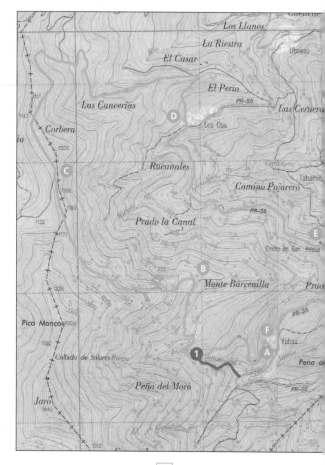

more conifers beyond which is a small open area. As the track ahead descends into sparse oak woods pass through a wire gate, point ❶, a few metres after which the alternative start path joins the track from the left.

Shortly after this gate an overgrown track rises up to the right, ignore this and continue on the main track slightly down, negotiate a patch of broom growing in the track, with the stream down to the left, and follow round a sharp right hairpin. Continue along this track up the hillside through sparse oak, broom and heather, for about a kilometre until you emerge into a hollow meadow on the far side of which, ahead of you, is a small invernale. ⓑ

At this point six large oak trees are on your left. Bear left past these across the meadow to pick up the track once more that now takes a very steep upward gradient for the next 250 metres, or so. Take care on the loose surface. As the gradient lessens, and you pass a large broom bush growing in the track, you will see the village of Los Cos down to your right. Continue ahead and up the track as it passes through more woodland and broom clumps until, after approximately another 1.5 kilometres, it emerges onto an open grassy ridge.

From here and for the next kilometre, or so, the track, switching from the left to the right side of the ridge, affords a virtual 360 degree panorama with stunning views across two valleys and to mountains beyond. This point is also an obvious place to stop for rest and refreshment.

Behind you in the distance lie Peña Ciquera, 'the Old Lady', and beyond the sloping table top above Puerto de Piedrasluengas. Ⓒ

Down and across to your right is the Liebana valley with its myriad villages. Ahead of you lies the massif of the Picos and down to the left is Valle de Cerceda carrying the road, CA-621, up to Puerto San Glorio, the far summit of which becomes more visible over your left shoulder as the walk progresses.

When, if ever, you have had enough of the views continue the walk by following the track ahead as it rises slightly, passing along the left of the unnamed conical peak at 1,206 metres, then crosses over to the right of the ridge and begins to descend. Looking down ahead is a transmitter mast on a hilltop and beyond this, in the distance, the great grey cliffs that form the portals of La Hermida gorge. The rough track now winds down the fairly open mountainside, steeply in places, for about a kilometre until it passes through a clump of broom. Immediately after this, at a left curve, another wide track forks down to the right; follow this soon taking a sharp right to pass a lone tree on the left. The track then rises briefly before descending once more. As you walk along the remainder of this track to Los Cos be on the lookout for a variety of bird life – especially great grey shrike that thrive in this habitat.

Taking a sharp left, just before a group of larch, the track fords a stream, Rio Román, and soon passes a row of nine, evenly spaced, mature cherry trees along the left. The rooftops of Los Cos appear on your right and, 100 metres or so, before some electricity pylons ahead, meet a 'crossroads'. Take the track that heads down sharply to the right. On the left, just before entering the village, is a small boarhound compound on the wall of which pairs

of sabots, the traditional wooden clogs of the region, are sometimes seen. Ⓓ

As you reach a grassy enclosure in front of the church, often used for grazing sheep, turn right and shortly come to a T-junction. Turn right and, as the concrete track expires to become rocky, head down. The track swings left and fords a stream. From here it is a fairly level, contour-following walk back to Yebas through mixed woodland.

Along this stretch in spring and summer you will encounter many types of woodland and water-loving plants, in particular, the vivid blue wild columbine. The authors have also seen pine marten here, so keep a look out.

At one point you may be forgiven for having déjà vu as the track again turns sharp left to ford another stream, on this occasion, however, there is a water trough on the right. After a few hundred metres pass a boomerang-shaped water trough on the right that bears a dedication plaque and soon after come to the Ermita de San Roque. Ⓔ Dropping down left to the front of this building takes you across the sandy bed of the bolero. The Ermita is usually locked but can be viewed through the grill in the door.

Leaving the Ermita continue along the track soon seeing, across the valley to your left, the village of Lerones (Walk 5) and ahead Yebas. As you pass grass fields to left and conifers to right enter the village where the track becomes concrete. Take the first steep road right passing on your right a barn seemingly overflowing with goats, the 'billy' often to be seen tethered at the top of the wooden steps above.

At the top of this road meet a T-junction. Right is where you began the walk, depending on the start option chosen. Turn left, passing under the house, and return down to your car.

views from a green ridge

Notes and observations

bees, parrots and an 'absei

Walk summary:

Distance: Approximately 10 kilometres
Time: Allow 3½ hours

Description: The inclusion of parrots in the title of this walk is somewhat tenuous referring as it does to a private aviary at Esanos and not the likelihood of spotting them in the wild! The reference to bees, however, is more germane. You will see beehives scattered in and around many villages in this region, often fashioned in the traditional manner from a hollowed tree trunk, but

Aviary at Esanos

here, as you drive past Pumareña and then Esanos, a great many are visible up on the hillsides to your left. The production and sale of honey is obviously a very important source of income to these three closely-neighbouring villages and also an indication of the abundance of flowers

San Pedro – Ermita de San Pedro de Toía – Salarzón – Sierra Cobeña – Pumareña – Esanos – San Pedro

Ermita

in spring and summer – even the village name board at San Pedro has a sign for 'miel' hanging beneath it.

The route encompasses an initial gradual ascent of around 450 metres tracking and crossing a rushing stream, then passing up through woodlands, the latter offering shade on a hot day. The first destination, while ostensibly an Ermita, is not apparently what it ought to be according to the map symbol.

The middle section is a gentle descent through sparse woods and meadows into the pretty village of Salarzón with its austere church. Beyond this it follows a ridge that ultimately provides good views over to the entrance of the Hermida gorge and the peaks beyond before descending finally to Pumareña, Esanos and back to San Pedro.

Driving directions

From Potes drive through Ojedo and follow the N-621 to Tama soon after which take the right turn signed to San Pedro. Park in the lay-by on the right, immediately before the village name sign and alongside the wide steps up to the cemetery.

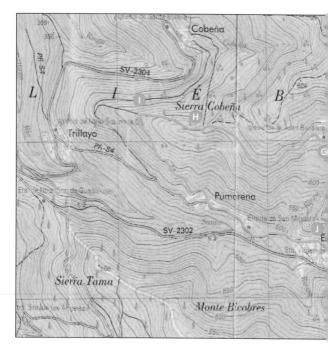

The walk

Cross the river bridge passing the San Pedro sign Ⓐ and shortly come to a newly built bus shelter on the right, behind which is the bolero, at which point the main road curves left to Salarzón. Take the concrete road heading off right leaving the village. After passing buildings, and crossing another river bridge where the concrete surface soon expires to become a rough track, pass bright green gates and begin to follow a stone wall on the left. Ⓑ

Over the next 1.5 kilometres, or so, the track climbs gently and pretty much straight ahead with a number of streams that pass either under or over the track, tumbling down from the woodland on the right. Reaching a water trough on the right the track forks, straight-ahead and curving round left. Follow the track left. After a few metres cross a bridge over the rushing

88

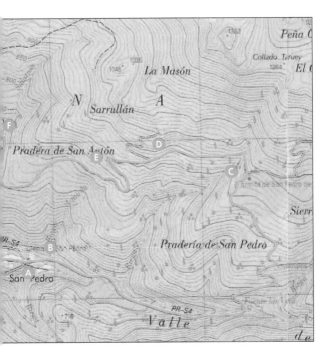

stream beyond which the track makes a sharp left and climbs passing on the right the gates to an apparently recently built 'summer' house. Follow the track up and after 100 metres, or so, with another track leading off ahead, continue round the sharp right hairpin. You are now walking through oak woods that, in terms of flora and fauna, are a delight in all seasons. Continue up on

the main track passing, at the apex of a left hairpin, an invernale to the right after which is a short dead end track off to the left along which will be many beehives in spring and summer but, sadly, may also be a derelict Land Rover. Continue up as the track makes a right hand hairpin past another invernale. Beyond this the gradient becomes less steep and after a kilometre, or so, come to a large walled meadow on the right, at the far side of which is a large invernale beside which is a much smaller, unseen building.

On reaching this site there should be, according to the most recent topographical maps, the Ermita de San Pedro de Toía. The authors can find no religious symbols, nearby information boards nor direction signs to indicate that the larger building is anything other than a livestock shelter. Equally, though, neither have they researched further, so once perhaps the Ermita was here or maybe the symbol on the map is simply erroneously placed.

Nonetheless, at this point are two white and yellow way mark signs, one on a concrete 'trig' the other on a small wooden post. C

The main track you have been following continues ahead but an equally wide track drops steeply down left. Take the latter and, after about 100 metres follow the track as it takes a sharp left crossing a stream. You are now walking above a wooded hillside to the left.

After another 700 metres, or so, at the confluence of a number of springs and streams, you will come to, what can only be described as a bizarre metal water 'cabinet' set into the hillside on the right from which water cascades leaving the track surface, unsurprisingly, river-like. D

Just past this, ignoring a wide grassy track forking off and up to the right, continue ahead, immediately passing a flat concrete slab with two circular inspection covers. At a point where tracked meadows are visible through the trees far down to your left you come to a junction where another track swings round and down sharp left. A few metres beyond this point a pair of concrete water troughs are set into the right side of the bank, above them is a painted white and yellow way marker. E

Take the track that swings down left and after about 5 minutes, at the point where another track joins down from the left, follow the right hairpin down. You are walking through open woodlands that soon give way, first on the left then right, to open meadows. Looking down left to the narrow meadows in the valley far below you will see, on the far side of these, the track you followed on the outward route from San Pedro. Soon after passing a huge concrete block water cistern the village of Salarzón comes into view ahead.

Walk down through woodland until you cross over a stream, Riega de Salarzón, on a rough wooden plank. **F**

Continue ahead until, passing the first (white) house on the left, the concrete road forks three ways through the village, take the lower left following it as it descends past railings and then turns left down beside the 1819 built church of San Juan Bautista de Salarzón. Although the church is locked it is worth entering the grassed area to the front of the starkly pillared entrance to see the fantastic locking door bolt. **G**

Standing beside the church, and facing the pink/orange railings, turn right and then right again up past the village potro, at which point there may also be a large pile of

firewood in the middle of the intersection, and take the concrete road left. Soon after leaving the village the concrete expires to become a muddy track passing a small wooden clapper-board building on the right with views down immediately left to vegetable plots and beyond to Esanos.

After this, and for the next kilometre, or so, the track continues ahead gently descending but mostly contour following and, ignoring all other joining tracks, passes close by a group of mature conifers on the left.

After a short section where the track becomes a footpath, passing low bramble hedges, it widens once again to meet a fork. The right track goes down to the village of Cobeña, just visible below. Ⓗ

At this point also a tree to the left of the track bears a clearly painted white and yellow way mark. Take the left and continue down. Soon Cobeña with its very modern church, isolated on the left of the village beside the main road, can be seen more clearly and beyond this views to the craggy entrance of La Hermida gorge. As the route descends the ridge and continues straight ahead, down toward wide open ground, another, less major but still quite wide, track swings off to the left, at which point a way mark sign is painted on a rock to the left and close to the ground. Take this left track, passing through scrubby broom, which soon emerges onto a small meadow, becomes grassy and passes just below a small group of mature conifers with the village of Trillayo seen down to your right. The track, continuing grassy then rocky, soon emerges into Pumareña.

As you meet the smooth tarmac road surface in the village 'centre' pass the water troughs on your left above which the village name is displayed and continue ahead right to follow the railings on your right, passing the bolero, until you reach the small Ermita. Beyond this is a bridge over the river that joins the main road. Turn left just before the bridge to follow the wide track up between walled vegetable allotments to the right and a stream to the left until you reach Esanos. On the hillside above you at this point are many beehives but these can only be viewed clearly from the main road, over to your right. ●

Pass close by a red brick house to the right, with an unusual fox and eagle chimney cowl, and take the upper road left between more traditional houses to reach a short, straight stretch of road with railings on your right. ● At the end of this turn left and take the upper road to San Pedro church, at which, passing to the right and emerge onto the main road and your car.

Notes and observations

legs a

Walk summary:

Distance: Approximately 9 kilometres
Time: Allow 3$\frac{1}{2}$ hours

Description: The title of this walk refers to the initial stiff ascent of about 280 metres over approximately 1.5 kilometres to Torices, passing the site of a former monastery, and then on the final stage of the descent, although mapped, the lack of track to follow.

Although there has been a church dedicated to San Martín on the site at Torices since 1075, much of the present building dates from the 16th century. The village is neat and contains two modern but sympathetic developments of holiday apartments, along with their well-appointed picnic areas. From here there is a more gradual ascent along hillside and through woodland before finally dropping back down through meadows to the road near Sana.

Driving directions

From Potes drive to Ojedo and turn right onto the CA-184. Soon after entering Puente Asnil, and just past the 6-kilometre marker, take the left turn signed to Lamedo.

initiative

After approximately 1.5 kilometres, below the unseen village of Sana up to the right, come to a large lay by on the left side of the road. Turn your car round and park here.

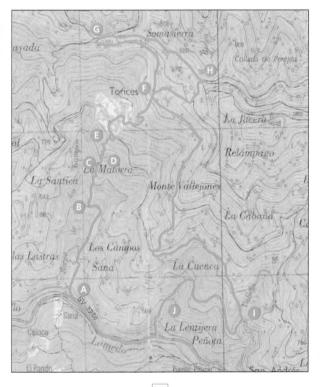

legs and initiative

The walk

Seen from your about-face position is a wide shale track heading up right from the lay by.  Ⓐ Follow this, soon passing a brightly liveried but wheel-less lorry trailer on the right. Continuing up the main track, and ignoring any going off to left and right, you will come, after 400 metres, or so, to a rust and pink gate bearing a dilapidated sign requesting that it be kept closed. Beyond this gate, ahead of you, is a large meadow that dips and then rises, at the far side of which is a very large and modern invernale and above and beyond this, at the far high end of the meadow, is a bright orange gate through which the route will pass.

Pass through the rusty gate, leaving it as you found it. Follow the rocky track ahead and half right that leads up briefly through woodland but soon emerges near the top right of the meadow. (N.B. After passing through this gate you could follow the track through the meadow ahead toward the invernale but this can be very muddy). Either way, cross the top of the meadow passing by the invernale down to your left and bearing left above it, Ⓑ briefly down then up, to the orange gate set in the hedge. Pass through this gate and immediately meet a wooded stony track running down from right to left. Turn right and follow this narrow, hollow and winding path as it rises steeply. You will come to a black and white rectangular sign, hanging somewhat incongruously from a small tree on the left of the path, that bears the bold legend *'Monasterio de Santa Cristina: bautizado el Rey Alfonso I';* shortly all will be revealed. Ⓒ

At this point the track meets a T-junction with a wider track running down from right to left; turn right and come, after a few metres, to a small, open grassy area on

the right. On the far side of this is a very large, white (and blue) cross ⓓ – beside which is a large piece of masonry along with a pile of railway sleepers. This is the site of the former monastery. Standing with the cross on your right look up to see, on the skyline ahead, the church at Torices – the next destination.

Leaving this site rejoin the track and follow it as it continues to rise steeply toward the church, passing a meadow to the left then taking a series of twists and turns between bramble hedges before finally emerging, most thankfully, onto a concrete road beside the church.

Turn left here and come to a picnic area with sturdy rustic seating. **E** This is worth a brief investigation for within it is a small stone shelter containing, not only a double barbecue and electricity supply but also, a sink with cold tap: an excellent place to replenish water supplies! Leaving this follow the concrete road into the village passing by the entrance gates to a very modern (holiday accommodation) development 'Viviendas rurales de Cantabria', to which the picnic site belongs. Turn right and soon meet a fork at which take the left. Ahead lies a water trough beside which is yet another well appointed picnic site.

Continue ahead passing the water trough and picnic site on your left and more modern 'Viviendas' with balconies. Immediately after these the road forks three ways; left, ahead and a hairpin that rises sharply round up to your right. Take the latter. After passing a house on the left, and with views down right to the rooftops of the village and church, the concrete expires and you are now following a tractor track. Continue, as it becomes a wide and winding rising track, until you reach a green-posted cattle grid. **F** At this point, to which you will return, there is a 'pinkish' gate to the right and an intersection of tracks. Follow the left track beyond the cattle grid that descends briefly and then follows a gentle upward left curve along the hillside. After 500 metres, or so, come to another intersection. First a level grassy track heads off right immediately beyond which is a T-junction where, to the left, is another pinkish gate and to the right the track runs down steeply through woodland. Ignore the two further tracks and take the first right, grassy, track. **G** After walking fairly level through woodland for 600 metres, or so, emerge onto a grassy area at a major intersection where clearly visible tracks join coming down from the hillside ahead and half left. **H** At this point take the right track as it descends past a large meadow on the

right, turns sharp right and then, after another 500 metres, or so, reaches the cattle grid passed earlier. Immediately before the cattle grid a track left bypasses it, beside the 'pinkish' gate. Follow this as it sweeps briefly up and then begins to descend gently following the contour of the hillside. 500 metres, or so, after a sharp right turn, the track rises slightly and then levels to meet a distinct fork.

Follow the right track as it begins to descend curving left. You are now following a wooded ridge with steep slopes to both sides. Soon, after passing between wooden posts, the track curves slightly right to follow the right side of the ridge. As you meet a T-junction with a grassy track, running down right and down left, turn left. After a kilometre, or so, the track, descending steeply with meadows and a large invernale over to the left, meets a distinct fork. Follow the track that continues down ahead half right. Soon, where the gradient becomes steeper, another invernale set into the woodland is ahead of you.

Reaching another fork where the track turns sharply left to ford a stream, and with a stone wall lying ahead bearing a left-pointing painted arrow, take the right upward track. ● Soon after passing a group of mature conifers on the left the track curves left across a steep meadow after which you will come to the first of 4 barbed wire/log fences. Pass through the first and follow the indistinct track as it crosses a meadow sloping down from right to left toward a fence, at the bottom left of which you will once again pick up the track as it drops ahead passing through another wood and wire gate.

The track, now no more than a wide grassy hollow through the meadow, passes through two more barbed wire 'gates' in quick succession and follows wooden enclosures to the left. Turn left past the end of these

enclosures heading down through the centre of a meadow. From this point there is virtually no path to follow – just keep going downhill!

As you head down the meadow keep to the left of a tall 'hedgerow' with dry streambed beneath. Soon, with a group of tall conifers 100 metres, or so, over to the left, come to a wide gap in the hedgerow on your right and pass through this, briefly picking up a track. Pass a tall conifer on the left, ignoring a narrow cattle track to the right rising up into woodland, and head down this second narrow meadow toward a small plantation of conifers surrounded by a sturdy wooden fence dead ahead. **J**

Continue down passing to the right of these toward a barbed wire fence ahead, at the extreme right of which is a 'gate'. At this point you will be able to just see the main road, and Armco, 200 metres, or so, below. Pass through this gate and continue down following the right side of the meadow. After 60, or so, metres a wide track mysteriously appears in the meadow; follow this as it abruptly disappears and then reappears to become a wide, steep, shale grit track which soon joins the main road. At this point turn right along the road to walk the kilometre, or so, back to your car.

legs and initiative

Notes and observations

ancient church, an

ancie

Walk summary:

Distance: Approximately 13 kilometres
Time: Allow 5 hours

Description: This route begins at the ancient Mozárabe church of Santa Maria de Lebeña; a beautiful building with its separate bell tower, well worth visiting to see its many artefacts – some dating from the 10th century. Open hours, are 10:00 to 13:30 and 16:00 to 18:00 other than Mondays and on religious festivals when it is closed. Ⓐ

From here there is short walk, retraced on the return, to nearby Allende and then a longer, more strenuous climb following a section of the renowned track toward the remote village of Bejes. From its highest point, an overall ascent of approximately 400 metres, just inside the national park the route drops through the villages of Cabañes and neighbouring Trascoba, thereafter crossing moorland before passing through the remnants of ancient chestnut woodland to return to Cabañes and then descend a woodland track back to Allende and Lebeña. The route benefits from two bars, a 'cider shop', all closed in winter, and a snack kiosk by the church at Lebeña. If you do not encounter Griffon vultures,

Lebeña – Allende –
Invernales de la Pelea –
Cabañes – Trascoba –
Castañera de Pendes –
Cabañes – Allende –
t **trees** Lebeña

sometimes at close quarters, on this route you will be very unlucky.

In summer this walk is ideally undertaken on a weekday with an early start to help avoid a busy car park at the church, picnickers near Cabañes and the midday sun.

Driving directions

From Potes drive to Ojedo and follow the N-621 through Tama. Soon after entering La Hermida gorge take the well signposted right turn toward Lebeña and then the left turn to the church where there is plenty of parking space.

ancient church and ancient trees

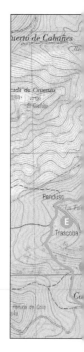

The walk

Leave the church and head back along the road to rejoin the N-621. Turn right and after crossing the road bridge come to the left turn to Allende opposite the 'Bar el Desfiladero'. To the left of the road, opposite the bus shelter, is a steeply rising concrete track that is the 'old' road to Allende. Follow this track as it rises, curving up below and then into the lower village, its surface varying between concrete, grit and grass en route. As it passes between buildings it soon emerges to meet the main road entering the village. Turn up left and, as you pass by an old building with a balcony, turn right and continue to reach a junction where the road ahead narrows between buildings and a road goes off right. You will come back to this point on the return journey. Close to the ground on the building in front of you is the white and yellow way mark, above which is a white right-pointing arrow. Follow this road right as it then curves left and begins to ascend first passing a pair of farm buildings, one of which is painted green, and then black and yellow signs warning of bees, beyond which are the hives. Ⓑ

You are now following a wide and distinct track that, shortly turning left, will continue upwards to the summit of the route taking about one and a half hours – depending on your ability and the temperature. Follow the main track, which is bordered intermittently on the left by a metal-posted wire fence, ignoring all other tracks heading off left and right. At one point, a wide track joins sharply down from the right beside which is a

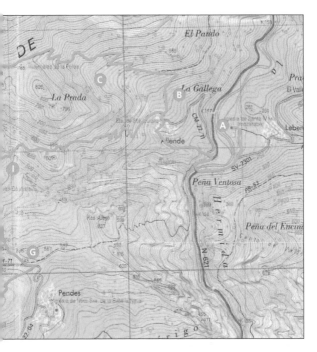

slightly misleading way mark sign. Ignore this and continue straight ahead and up keeping the metal posted fence to the left; noting that here two of the narrow fence posts bear crudely painted upward-pointing white

arrows with a bolder one painted on a rock to the right of the track just beyond. Down to your left will be seen a few invernales one of which, beside a group of poplars looks for all the world as if it has landscaped terraced 'lawns'. C

The track makes two right and left hairpins before straightening a little to make a final zigzag sequence passing close by the first and then second of the Invernales de la Pelea. Beyond these, as the gradient lessens then levels, the track becomes concrete and passes a large, walled meadow with another neat invernale on the left and soon meets a major intersection at which are walkers' signposts; the right track signed to Bejes.

Take the track ahead signed to Cabañes D that soon curves left and rises slightly to cross a cattle grid from which point, the highest of the route, you will begin descending a steep and winding concrete road. Shortly after passing by a television receiver station the track reaches the 'main' road in Cabañes. Turn right to pass a wooden built cider shop and then the church. Follow

this level road toward the village of Trascabo, seen approximately 800 metres ahead. As the main road turns sharp left follow the concrete road, beside a wooden sign for 'Penduso', which rises steeply to the right. Just after passing the large, modern restaurant bar 'Las Guindales' **E** come to a three way fork in the village and continue ahead. The road descends gently and after passing the last house on the right, with black railings, the concrete expires and you will be on a wide rough track that soon fords a stream, Arroyo de la Mata, turns sharp left and rises up through woodland. Continue up and roughly straight ahead, ignoring all tracks rising right and dropping left, for about 500 metres, or so, until you emerge from the woods onto open moorland of scattered gorse, heather and bracken at which point a wide grassy track heads off right toward a nearby hill with rocky summit. **F** Continue on the track ahead for 250 metres, or so, as it descends into a dip, passes above a cattle trough on the left and fords a small stream. At this point the track becomes a little indistinct but turn half left and continue ahead and up and, after a couple of minutes, you will meet a T-junction with a distinct vehicle track running gently down from right to left. Turn left and follow this track as it passes to the right of the hillside, with views into the Valle de Cillorigo and the village of Tama far below on the right, and then crosses a cattle grid beside a small sports pitch to join the main road. Here you will pass by the first group of massive pollarded chestnut trees. On reaching the road turn left for a few metres and cross over into the open picnic area.

You are now among the Castañera de Pendes. ⓖ This tiny area of Spain, between the villages of Cabañes and Pendes, has the largest remaining concentration of these centuries-old trees that once covered the hillsides – there is another smaller group in the village of Pesaguero, near to the start of walk 5. The largest of these huge sentinels has a girth of 14 metres and in winter, when the branches are bare, they take on a strange anthropomorphic appearance.

To continue the walk you will now follow a short, unmapped track back to Cabañes. Facing the stone-built barbecue turn left taking the wide track, passing the large paved parking area on your left. This track now descends through a large grove of chestnut trees first turning right then left to meet a fork. At this point take the left that continues down to re-cross the Arroyo de la Mata on a wooden footbridge, ⓗ then follow the stony track up to meet a T-junction with a concrete road; at which turn right to re-enter Cabañes. Turn right through the village and, at the 'Albergue' sign, descend half right passing a large modern breeze-block farm building on your right. The concrete expires to become a rough track that after 200 metres, or so, and passing a 'Picos gate' halfway across the track, ⓘ fords a stream.

At this point, by a wooden finger post pointing back to the monastery of Santo Toribio, the track forks three ways. Take the steep rocky track rising half right ahead into woodland that, after crossing a small grassy area,

then descends and winds along the right of the hillside for just over a kilometre. As you reach the concrete road at Allende turn right and soon come to the point where you began the main ascent. From here retrace your steps back down through the village to the N-621 at the Bar el Desfiladero and then to the church at Lebeña.

Notes and observations

a prehisto

Walk summary:

Distance: Approximately 8.5 kilometres
Time: Allow 2½ hours

Description: After an initial ascent of approximately 160 metres, to its highest point above Panes, this walk is mostly a pleasant stroll although for a short stretch, beyond the church at Cimiano, the track can be very muddy. The route passes through an area of once ancient forest then by the cave entrance at La Loja, near El Mazo, before following the fen-like Rio Deva valley to return to Panes. As you walk it is easy to see, given the once dense forest, the resources of the Rio Deva and its fertile valley coupled with the shelter of nearby limestone caves, why this was one of the earliest inhabited regions of northern Spain.

At 100 metres long La Loja is one of a number of 'minor' caves in the region and, as with all others for reasons of preservation, accepts a maximum number of visitors, in its case 35 per day. The jewel within the cave is a roughly metre square 'panel' of c15,000 year-old Palaeolithic artwork depicting cattle and a horse. While this and other symbols in the cave are clearly historically important, they are somewhat visually indistinct and may

Panes – Cimiano – El Argayo 'forest' – La Loja cave (El Mazo) – Vega de Siejo – Río Deva – Panes

route

disappoint those expecting an Altamira-like masterpiece. Nonetheless, both the images and history of the cave are fascinating and should you wish to visit it is necessary to make an advance reservation at the information centre beside the entrance to the cave.

Driving directions

From Potes drive to Ojedo to follow the N-621 through La Hermida gorge to Panes. There are 'hard shoulders' as you enter the town offering plenty of parking.

a prehistoric route

The walk

Assuming that you have parked soon after entering the town, walk ahead along the main road to turn right along the road signed to the 'Plaza' and after a few metres the large church lies ahead. Continue on the road to the right of the church as it passes the new plaza on the left and soon meets a crossroads at which are zebra crossings. Cross the road to continue ahead between buildings on a level road, neatly paved with pale bricks, for a short distance until the surface becomes concrete and, with stone walls either side, meet a fork. Take the left and as you pass the last buildings the surface becomes grass and rock and begins to ascend. The track curves round right following electricity lines above you for a short distance. After passing a small boarhound enclosure, it levels to pass a concrete wall on the right after which it climbs left.

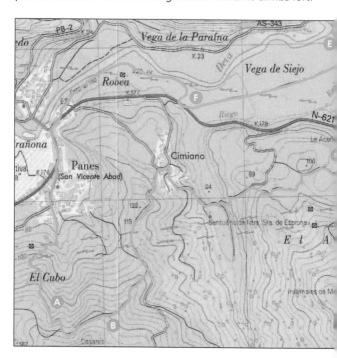

Here are the first good views down left to Panes and its impressive new road bridge over the Rio Deva. **A**

Continue into eucalyptus woodlands passing, on the left, the entrance to a very neat house bounded by a leylandii hedge along the left of the track. As the wide track emerges from the eucalyptus it begins to descend. You are now walking through an area that once was the dense El Argayo forest. **B**

After 10 minutes, or so, meet a fork where the concrete road left goes down to Panes. Take the right and follow this to Cimiano passing a very grand house on the way to the village.

Continue down left on tarmac surface to meet a T-junction, at which is a small recreation area and bolero, and turn right. Walk through the village passing a central vegetable patch on the left and, as the road curves right, pass a blue painted house on the right opposite which is a 3 metre high concrete bell tower.

Continue between these and where the road forks take the descending concrete road left to pass a water trough and farm buildings. At another fork take the left and shortly you will see a small isolated church a short distance down ahead of you. Cross a bridge over the stream immediately ahead of the church, keeping an eye out for warblers in the nearby bushes. The church bears an information plaque describing its refurbishment and ahead of you is a group of large stone-built seats and tables set into the hillside, just here the track forks.

Take the left that rises and becomes very muddy as soon as the concrete expires. Follow this up through a

few twists and turns until it levels onto a firm surface and passes an invernale just over to the left to meet another very distinctive fork. Take the right and soon pass an electricity pylon and then a meadow bounded by a sturdy fence made of railway sleepers on the right and then, on the left, a large farmyard building the enclosure of which is made of Armco! Continue ahead passing under a 10 metre high rock face as the track swings left, crosses a stream, and then joins a main road beside an invernale. Walk ahead down this road to meet the N-621. As you walk down this stretch note the white house down to your left around which runs a tarmac road bearing white lines. This is a twisting section of the 'old' road from Unquera to Panes. Ⓒ

At the N-621 turn left and cross over and soon meet a concrete road dropping left by a garage and other buildings. At this point there is a notice board and finger post for La Loja cave. Ⓓ

Take this road as it soon curves right and heads toward the village of El Mazo. A hundred metres or so before the village take the concrete road left toward a group of white buildings and soon after these, just before a wide stream ditch, take the right toward the buildings at the entrance of the cave.

Once at this building, and its small entry kiosk, unless you are visiting the cave there is little else to see other than the barred metal gate covering the entrance to the cave 4 metres, or so, up on the limestone face. To the left of the main building runs a narrow path.

Follow this beside the stream to reach a wide bend in the Rio Deva, on the other side of which is a small building above, what looks like, the concrete 'wharf' of a lido. Ⓔ

Take care here – the path is narrow and the river currents strong. Make your way back on the path past the cave entrance and along the concrete road to rejoin the main 'road' and turn right over the bridge to begin walking across the flat plain of the Vega de Siejo. This large tract of land, which must be very fertile, seems strangely uncultivated save for grass and a few strips of maize. As this concrete road eventually rises to meet the N-621 just below Cimiano you have a choice. **F** Either join the N-621 and follow it the kilometre, or so, back to Panes, or take the continuing stony track which, while running alongside the river, will entail crossing two awkward

fences across the route; the authors believe these ought really to be gates.

If you choose the latter route continue on the track as it descends turning right then left to pick up a shallow and fast running stretch of the Rio Deva – a haven for dippers. Soon after entering woodland come to a track heading off right through the trees to a stony 'beach'. Ignore this and continue ahead to meet a wire fence that you must either pass under or through to enter a small rough pasture. Once through head to the far left corner to reach a dense pile of brushwood among which is a

roughly constructed hurdle fence. At this point you may see lorries parked in a depot up to your left. Cross this hurdle fence and continue ahead on a distinct track as it curves past an orchard on your left to meet a T-junction, at which turn right and soon emerge onto the N-621 by a petrol station. Continue along the road a short distance to come into Panes.

a prehistoric route

Notes and observations